DEDICATION

To entrepreneurs; the front liners and many yet unsung.

CONTENTS

Foreword

Acknowledgements

Introduction

FOREWORD

From Prof. Pat Utomi

A good old Christian chorus announces that 'all over the world the spirit is moving'. Reading 'Ola Grace manuscript on the *Our Entrepreneurship Mandate* leaves me that same warmth of feeling, seeing a young Nigerian woman so strongly moved by the spirit of Enterprise to provide her generation both an Entrepreneurship cookbook and a motivation to venture volume. All over the text the spirit seemed in ascent and motion.

Writing simply and informedly she traverses a landscape I have engaged students on in MBA classes at the Lagos Business School for two decades now. Her choice to bring and African prism to the window from which she looks at the subject matter makes it even more relevant and valuable for a continent that needs to urgently promote entrepreneurship to lift the debilitating veil of poverty and slow economic growth.

Exploring the challenge of material advance in Africa, she poses the rhetorical question: Is Africa hopeless; then she goes on to domicile the solution at the feet of 'political will'. But as I have argued many times it is the absence of that political will which makes a developmental state less likely, that makes entrepreneurship imperative, if progress is to be claimed.

I welcome the author's insight and simple style as part of fanning new fires of venturing that need to become the emblem of this generation if the population growth on the continent of Africa is to become a demographic dividend and not a population time bomb.

Fondly called Professor Pat Utomi (born February 6, 1956), he is a Nigerian professor of political economy and management with the Lagos Business School (ranked among the Best Business Schools in the World) Pan Atlantic University, Lagos.

He is a Fellow of the Institute of Management Consultants of Nigeria and a former presidential candidate. He is the founder of Centre for Value in Leadership (CVL) and the African Democratic Congress party. He has served in senior positions in government, as an adviser to the president of Nigeria, the private sector, as Chief Operating Officer for Volkswagen of Nigeria and in academia with several publications, and a most sought-after public speaker across the globe.

From Dr. Chance M. Glenn, Sr.

The rapid cycle of technology has caused transition around the globe. The world is connected and the time required to go from concept to product has shortened considerably. This paves the way for opportunity and there are many who realize this and are taking advantage of it. *Our Entrepreneurship Mandate* not only captures the significance of the opportunity, but also emphasizes the necessity, particularly for the country of Nigeria. As an African-American citizen, with roots that lead back to West Africa, my personal hopes and dreams for my motherland are for it to thrive and for our people to enjoy to fruits of enormous potential that resides there.

'Ola-Grace does a magnificent job in capturing the concept and power of building business from the ground up. She challenges the leadership of the country to step forward and provide the seeds of growth that they have access to, thus creating a legacy that will last long beyond their tenures. She makes it clear that while being innovative, placing entrepreneurship centrally within public policy is the best way to transform a society for the better.

While this book is an important piece in advising decision-making in Nigeria, it is also a speaks to those from outside of Nigeria who may seek to do business there. There is an impressive level of insight incorporated into this book, and those who read it will come away wiser than when they began. Kudos to 'Ola-Grace for bringing this important subject to the forefront.

Dr. Chance M. Glenn, Sr. is a tenured full professor and the Dean of the College of Engineering, Technology and Physical Sciences at Alabama

A&M University in the United States.   He holds a Ph.D. in Electrical Engineering from the Johns Hopkins University and a Management Development Certificate from the Graduate School of Education at Harvard University. He is also the founder and President of Morningbird Media Corporation, which publishes and develops multimedia for worldwide distribution.

ACKNOWLEDGEMENTS

Writing this book, my thoughts and insights do not in any way diminish the imprints of several years of external influences on the overall value of the work: I have over the years learnt from books, people, events and personal experiences. And so when it was time to write this book, I simply let the thoughts flow unfettered.

I attribute most of my inspiration to reading, and over the years, I have found much joy and inspiration from the works of countless authors that have continued to inspire me till date.

The many tunnels in my life adventures were made easier by the books that kept me company; fiction and nonfiction alike, all weaving the intricate tapestry of my eclectic disposition.

Without authors there would be no readers. I salute the courage and resilience of men and women far and near that pay the price of enhancing knowledge, literacy and interests.

My family and friends remain invaluable in my pursuit and I owe much gratitude to them for the love and joy that makes life worth expressing.

To all the institutions, schools, professionals, tutors, mentors, leaders, colleagues, friends and protégés that have enhanced my appreciation of entrepreneurship, I hope we continue to build together, especially for the emancipation of Africa.

I acknowledge above all, the ultimate inspiration, the source of all ideas and purposes, and stay true to my veneration.

INTRODUCTION

Our Entrepreneurship Mandate is Afrocentric for the dire need; Africa more than any part of the world has a huge socioeconomic burden and the urgency to meet the need behooves more than ever. As the figures continue to count negatively against Africa on all development indicators, Africa can and should do more than wish off the challenges.

Africa falls short in quality of life, life expectancy, infrastructure, literacy and human development, access to water and sanitation, quality of healthcare at all levels, while suffering from pervasive degradation across all sectors.

While there is a leadership responsibility, no doubt, to resolving the deficits, there is also an individual responsibility that I see with entrepreneurial development. Entrepreneurship holds the power to empower individuals to break off poverty like no other endeavor. When citizen are empowered to make money and create wealth, there is a ripple effect across other interests. With more income, comes increase in nutrition and health, increase in Human Development pursuits, overall economic development, and social inclusion. There is also a louder demand for good governance and improvement in development parameters.

Our Entrepreneurship Mandate moves entrepreneurship from a discretionary list of governments to obligatory. There must be an obligation on governments across the continent and elsewhere to prioritize entrepreneurship development if any meaningful socio-economic progress would be made in Africa.

The book has 3 practical parts to guide entrepreneurs, policymakers and all diverse interests in the transition from institutionalized corporation-driven macro-economies to start-up business driven economies, which now generate the most employment and new wealth in recent years.

While the emphasis of the book is on Africa, there is yet a global inflection that is needful against the reality that businesses in these times pervade national borders using the power of the internet.

Africa cannot work in isolation, entrepreneurial development in Africa must address local and international dynamics; it must cater for the illiterate women in the villages as well as the teeming youths in the urban centers.

As another era unfolds a global development agenda, Africa must sharpen the tools of entrepreneurship to enjoy the full benefits of an economically empowered people.

A Prototype Entrepreneurship Center suggests a workable model for grassroots mobilization.

The Post Script: The Nouveau Preneur Age adds a new opinion, rightly acknowledging the new breed of entrepreneurs and their important role in galvanizing the Digital age for gains.

The Perspectives put forth are 100% my thoughts and views, shaped by several years of practical exposure to study, research and endeavors in Entrepreneurship.

'Ola Grace

PART 1

PROEM

Enough cannot be said on Africa's urgency to focus on intensive and comprehensive entrepreneurship development as inevitable, if Africa is to make any significant ascent from the doldrums of underdevelopment and poverty. The need is more pressing now with the changing global economic realities and the challenges of the Climate Change.

As more wealth is being generated globally, the realities of inequality in wealth distribution also brings a new twist to the game: it is now official that 99% of global wealth is controlled by 1% of the world population (That is not hard to accept where over 500 hundred individuals are global billionaires and some countries cannot boast of $1Billion GDP debt-free).

With about 1 billion people still living under extreme poverty conditions globally and several billions managing to scale the mark (Africa and South Asia bearing the most poverty burden globally), there is more urgent need to address the socio-economic issue of wealth creation and income generation with entrepreneurship as the most important catalyst.

Entrepreneurship is a very stimulating discipline with tremendous potentials to transform individuals, communities and societies at large.

Entrepreneurs infuse new perspective to living and altogether sustain the new global economic verve. Win or lose; they are the brains and force behind much of the dynamism that the recent world is experiencing.

Entrepreneurship has evolved strongly in recent times and edged its way into the mainstream of most economies. While entrepreneurship itself is not new in practice, the word and body of knowledge it has recently harnessed is contemporary.

Entrepreneurship is good in all its ramifications: it creates jobs, creates wealth, a new economic order, and encourages personal congruence; and invariably a more productive world.

The urgency to understand, embrace, develop and propagate entrepreneurship more than ever stems from the yearning to address the global concerns addressed in the Sustainable Development Goals (SDGs). Africa bears the weight of the developmental deficits and the development goals might remain unattainable if we do not harness the resources and knowledge so far gotten to avoid another defeat as was largely the Millennium Development Goals (MDGs) in most of Africa (my view).

Economic empowerment of the people holds the key to unlocking much of the other goals, with entrepreneurship pivotal in our quest.

Much of the improvement that the world, particularly Africa will experience will be a lot dependent on the extent to which entrepreneurship and other productive endeavors can be harnessed soon and in the near future.

The eras of mass labor, man-power intensive corporations, over-bloated public service are gone. Rather than dissipate energy trying to reverse the tides, we must quickly realize, understand, harness and deploy all resources to take advantage of the move to entrepreneurship and start-up enterprises to accelerate meaningful development.

Judging from where most nations stand, it is safe to conclude that the extent to which individuals, organizations, and societies were able to take advantage of past economic eras have till date influenced wealth distribution globally. Africa missed out the most, and it is evident till date in the pervasive underdevelopment that dots the continent. The ships of plantation and feudal economies have sailed and berthed long ago, same as the industrial revolution (machine based industry) and mining boom to a large extent leaving Africa stranded on the shores of underdevelopment and despondency. ICT still has a lot to offer, but more of it will rest on entrepreneurs and not large corporations or government participation.

In spite of the past successes of developed countries, the race for continued growth and economic development remains the pursuit of all as the world population exceeds seven billion and the new direction in global development for sustainability with the urgent need to reverse the negative carbon effects on the environment while still pursuing economic and social well being.

The United States, in an unprecedented sweep, boasts of over 1000 Billionaire people and entities; with a commendable number owing to startup companies of less than 20 years. The startup effect trickles down to other numerous folks making very decent 6-digit incomes and employing millions in that clime and other developed nations, and a handful in Africa.

Africa must actively and proactively join this new dispensation to find succor in entrepreneurship which has proven to be a viable economic order that accommodates great and small businesses of all diversities. The underpinning of entrepreneurship does not require a certain skill set, capital requirement, location or interests. It just requires that you be able to create an income generating idea with whatever means or concept.

Entrepreneurship offers a fascinating sublime that connects folks of all variations to fulfill personal needs as well as collective interest: Madam Nike Davis-Okundaye, Africa's foremost textile designer with minimal education was able to project her passion to the global stage, today she is a resource person in Art Schools all over the world in spite of her humble beginning and limited education; such is the power of entrepreneurship.

Entrepreneurship remains the most amenable economic order to tackle unemployment, poverty, illiteracy, diseases, youth restiveness and many challenges currently being addressed in isolation. Much of the solution is with effective entrepreneurship development; with entrepreneurship comes more income, and with more income; improved standard of living, and a sense of social inclusion, which will substantially improve health, education, infrastructure and all.

Africa, particularly Nigeria has no business relying heavily on Official Development Aid (ODA) and philanthropy, with such vibrant and young population, arable land mass, extensive mineral deposit, forest resources, rich heritage and several advantages, yet unexplored.

It is only by infusing an entrepreneurship culture in the teeming populace that we can unlock the obscure, massive potentials in agriculture, science and technology, manufacturing, ICT, Food Processing & Packaging, Mining, Marine Economy, hospitality and tourism, entertainment and several latent multi- billion Dollar industries in Africa.

There was a time when communities built industries for the people, but now entrepreneurship reverses the order, with individuals creating businesses for the society, even making a new community as we see with Facebook, Uber and so many other ICT based new ideas.

The concept of Air BnB has grown from its American root to over 190 countries in a space of 7 years, becoming another Billion Dollar idea in that league. With no investments in Real Estates, it has made unprecedented impact in hospitality and travel experience.

I cannot emphasize enough that as Africa takes another swing at economic emancipation, entrepreneurship development should be a major focus for all who have genuine desire to see Africa and the underdeveloped world rise from debilitation and acquiescent dependency.

Entrepreneurship in Africa must first address basic challenges: Africans must be able to feed, clothe, shelter, and access clean water, sanitation, health care, basic education and essentials through home grown industrial efforts and economic activities that would foster sustainable development.

Africa must do all to ensure prosperity, peace, safety and development within her borders as a precursor to ensuring lasting economic progress. Insurgencies and insecurity will in no small measure undermine any attempt at economic prosperity: we cannot continue to devastate and ravage our home and run elsewhere for succor. It is a most dishonorable path which Africa must stem before it can see meaningful development.

If I may ask, is Africa hopeless? This question is to ponder and for introspection.

In my own view: Certainly not, I believe that meaningful change is attainable in Africa, solely dependent on us.

Singapore, China, UAE and much of Asia offers recourse that purposeful leadership, concerted efforts and a will to succeed is potent.

There must be a political will, political re-engineering and a concerted effort to forge and build an Africa for the people of Africa, drawing copious from success stories around and understanding the failings of previous attempts. We must ask the right question and answer openly and honestly. We can ask ourselves: Where are the doctors, administrators, engineers and professional that were sponsored on state scholarship abroad in the last 20 years? Very few have come back because the standards and infrastructure here do not even justify the trainings or encourage their return to the comatose economy.

How do we finance our development pursuits and cut back illicit financial flows? How do we move from an aid dependent economy to self-sufficiency? The assistance Africa gets from other nations and well-meaning individuals remain invaluable but the reality remains that only Africans can effectively build Africa; and sustainable change is only attainable by and in Africa.

Our land, water, and manpower in all respect must be maximally developed and utilized with effective framework for entrepreneurship development. The figures are tilting towards Africa in the next 30 years to supply the active workforce of the world, but that cannot be attained without qualitative human development in the continent.

Nigeria, South Africa, Egypt, Ghana, Kenya can spearhead the much needed drive on the continent to achieve the much needed economic revolution. South Africa has managed to scale over to the league of new developing countries classified as the BRICS (Brazil, Russia, India, China, and South Africa), but the burden of poverty in Africa, particularly in the other 48 Sub-Saharan African countries remains very critical and must continue to be a concern of all especially with the new global direction in collaborative development.

Economic development in Africa must take recourse to the convergence that has helped among the rest of the world: one country makes progress and the others soon fall in line to understand, adopt and imbibe the advancement. It must be appreciated that development at every point has never be congregated, but often spearheaded in a country with others inculcating the success model into their own clime.

Africa can indeed adopt and develop a template for economic development, set in the mould of entrepreneurship.

PRACTICAL INSIGHTS IN ENTREPRENEURSHIP DEVELOPMENT

Learning, teaching, researching and practicing entrepreneurship about two decades has been a most fulfilling and exhilarating experience.

In spite of the bumps and ditches, I remain an *entrepreneuraholic* (excuse my coinage). Days, months and even years of toil and sweat of an entrepreneur get paid for in one moment; and all the tension and pain diffuses into glee. For some of us – *entrepreneurholics*, we are just in transit as we move on to the next gritting experience lost in the frost of our quest for that break which may come, or never come; regardless we just keep forging on, with a firm resolve in the deep-set pursuit for an aha moment.

Entrepreneurship is as old as man. From the moment man set out to trade his surplus for his scarcity, man switched on his entrepreneurial mode and there has been no going back.

Entrepreneurship far reaches into prehistoric times in practice; though relatively new as a body of knowledge and discipline. The enterprising nature of man is what birthed most of the inventions, innovations and advancements we now enjoy, and the same has continued to fuel man's unquenchable desire for something more, bigger, new, better, different, improved and all the reasons why we have a constant flux, with more wealth being created, generated and harnessed across diverse endeavors, interests and enterprises.

Entrepreneurship development mirrors the socio-economic psyche of any societies, thriving with the inclinations of the people: wherever the folks are more daring, more ambitious, more curious, new economic activities soon sprung; little wonders that the more enterprising societies have more to show for.

In years past, entrepreneurship has never been regarded in the mainstream of economic policies, with most governments paying little attention in that direction. In recent times however, with resounding successes by entrepreneurs in all endeavors, there is a strong drive to reposition entrepreneurship as a core economic concern in all progressive economies. Entrepreneurs have bailed several nations from impending economic recesses, creating millions of jobs globally, reinventing ideas and overhauling conventional industries, thereby creating huge wealth and sustaining the whole process of socio-economic development in the 21st century. What seemed like a pretty good alternative some years back has become more than an alternative, edging its way to the main stream of discerning economies.

It is true that strong or weak entrepreneurial drive of a people impacts considerably on the overall well-being of the people as can be deduced in developed and underdeveloped societies. Even in Africa, many rural communities with high commercial activities have emerged to be Political power centers in the new nation-states that now make up the African continent. Commerce and trade was a foremost contributing factor to creation of big cities attesting to my realization that most big societies, even here in Africa boast of a vibrant commercial presence – Lagos, Ashanti Kingdom, Cairo, Addis Ababa, Kano Johannesburg, Nairobi, Onitsha and the likes.

Now that global policy attention is shifting to entrepreneurship as a viable economic order, Africa must do all to ensure that extreme poverty is eradicated in the coming years deploring the effective tool of entrepreneurship.

At the turn of the current political dispensation in Nigeria, heads of governments, policy Makers and all stakeholders emphasized the need to focus on youth empowerment, job creation and poverty alleviation; an emphasis well founded, given a country of over 170 million, with over 70% of our population within the active population bracket, and well over 70% of that group unproductive or underproductive. The importance of vibrant entrepreneurship development must be well articulated and not just remain sweet campaign promises.

As the focus on entrepreneurship grows, so also the studies and interest, particularly as it offers a ready palliative to millions who would otherwise have been unproductive or underproductive since big corporations are downsizing and governments are privatizing.

Any economy that can create 1 million entrepreneurs who also employ 2 or more other people is on its way to realizing its socio-economic objectives faster. In fact, there is a lot yet to be done as long as there are folks in the world who survive below the poverty-line ($1.90 per day), particularly in helping the under skilled and uneducated who have limited prospects in the formal sectors (entrepreneurship accommodates all leanings), and those who for the sheer love of ingenuity simply wish to start a new path for themselves and many others to follow.

Entrepreneurship is so significant in our times, where technology has taken up much of the jobs which were done by humans, and artificial intelligence is being developed, which will further reduce human inputs needed in productions. On the other side of the divide are developing countries grappling with poverty, hunger, diseases and high illiteracy in dire need of socio-economic impetus that only entrepreneurship offers in abundance.

My journey in entrepreneurship as a discipline and body of knowledge began at the turn of the millennium, a mentor and dear friend brought me on a project he undertook for the Federal Government, with the agency vested with SMEs development in Nigeria. The opportunity offered me the first glimpse of entrepreneurship as a discipline, which I had hitherto practiced for many years without understanding of the scope, principles and underpinnings. My foray later took me through many remote towns and villages, especially in the core Northern Nigeria: though languages and cultures differed, but our basic humanity was essentially the same with the cities.

While on an assignment, I met women in Daura, who had the same concerns as those in Osogbo, and Aba; how to cater for their families, particularly their children, essentially the same as was in Lagos and Abuja though the intensity differed.

The scanty economic activities in many of the remote communities invariably affected their capacity to generate reasonable income and the low human capital development activities held most bound and unproductive which I soon discovered that many of these folks are actually sitting on goldmines (rich loam soils, enormous mineral deposits, water bodies, ample land resources, cheap labor and other untapped or underutilized potentials) , but are too weak and oblivious to galvanize without meaningful impetus from external assistance; as put by Prof. Jeffery Sachs, they are stuck in a poverty trap.

I only began to understand and appreciate the poverty trap and its repressive tendencies which has become a debilitating influence in many rural communities over time while taking a Short Course- The Age of Sustainable Development by Prof. Jeffery Sachs, and all the puzzle fell into place as I realized that most of the folks must be deliberately unleashed from the jaws of poverty, which to them has become an alter ego.

On an assignment to the beautiful town of Wara in Kebbi State left me breathless: Wara, was one of the rural lush, and beautiful places I have been, with the tributaries of the River Niger adorning the town, with stretches of uncultivated Hectares of land, while the people languished in abject poverty. I was moved to tears when we located a Chinese settlement in that remote village that had taken advantage of the water bodies, next-to-free land, and excessive cheap labor, to create a most cost effective farmstead. The issues replicate in much of Africa, where many are languishing in abject poverty (economic and mind poverty) amidst the endowments of Mother Nature. Yes, there are real challenges in Africa, but most are opportunities waiting to be harnessed or modified.

Much of the inertia was fostered by economic policies that sapped initiative from individuals, while reposing the full responsibility for socio-economic development in the government. There is no doubt that there must be a significant change in this bid: It is good that attention is now shifting to entrepreneurship development and it is imperative that it must be done with long term impact as the main objective.

As many individuals, households, communities, nations and policy makers seek to leverage on entrepreneurship, there is need to contextualize and develop feasible models from the grassroots, if sustainable progress would be made.

In deploying entrepreneurship, there is need to also appreciate that there are undercurrents which may militate against the attainment of the ideals, varying with places and circumstances.

Developing Entrepreneurship is not as mundane as it may appear, as I found out on different assignments and from studying other projects. We are often confronted with the troubling reality that many of the people were not even as conscious about their challenges as we were, and they have become one with their miseries. We may carry out a feasibility study, brainstorm, find solutions and create ideas to emancipate poverty-ridden communities, do a Needs Analysis and develop bespoke concepts, but discover that the interests and values of the people may differ, making implementation difficult; often requiring a change in strategy.

The World Bank Group, The United Nations through its agency, The UNDP, USAid, DFiD, and several international bodies and private NGOs have gone up with trucks, personnel and funding to villages with empowerment projects in the bid to jumpstart micro-economic activities only to be barred by superstitions, apathy or even the obvious indifference.

Sometimes grant is given for start-up, and on the next return for assessment, the man has married a 15 year old girl, and there is no business to show but more malnourished children.

I applaud the efforts of these humanitarians, who in spite of several frustrated efforts, poor infrastructure, and the perils of impending attacks continually devise ingenious ways to make impact especially as I have seen in rural Nigeria.

Regardless of any challenges experienced, entrepreneurship remains the solution to unemployment, poverty, and several other socio-economic problems, as it continues to evolve into an empirical field of endeavor. The advantages outweigh the challenges and we must not be tempted to throw the baby with the bathwater; as we have done with the educational system, health and other sectors. We should concentrate on the overwhelming benefits that inures rather than the challenges.

This Book, *Our Entrepreneurship Mandate* offers practical insight as I have gathered from the fields and in my sojourn in the world of entrepreneurship. It is 100% my ideas, no portion culled or paraphrased from any writing. My views have been shaped on the field; learning, teaching and practicing this all important subject. As an unrepentant bibliophile, I have read loads of books and works on numerous subjects, and when it was time to piece these thoughts, I simply allowed my understanding and years of pupilage to flow through.

Might I conclude this Insights thus: entrepreneurship is like a Rose Plant: You get the thorns before the blossom; you must continue to water it until it blooms. But once its blooms, all the years of labor would be well compensated.

A QUICK GUIDE FOR ENTREPRENEURS

A book on entrepreneurship without hands-on application may be missing on essentials. To this extent, the Quick Guide for Entrepreneurs is expected to provide workable templates for existing and would-be entrepreneurs.

As much as I hope this would not sound too academic, the urge to define entrepreneurship subsists; the need to offer some sort of definition stems from an error that I have observed in this part of the world: I am much concerned that entrepreneurship has been so whittled down to vocational training especially in Africa, omitting several service-based, technology & ICT entrepreneurs among others. Youth Empowerment and Entrepreneurship are now interchangeably adopted for skill acquisition trainings.

Entrepreneurship is more than skills acquisition: it is not a game of small players, existing on the sideline of socio-economic realities. Entrepreneurship is both great and small with underlying principles that expands with the scope of operations. Entrepreneurship is a Billion Dollar as well as a few hundred or less. Entrepreneurship is set on the principles of Risk Bearing, Opportunity Grabbing and New ventures.

I would define Entrepreneurship as being able to create a sustainable stream of income through a venture, with such venture meeting a human need, and generating income that is able to sustain the venture and the owner as guided by the society frameworks.

An entrepreneur sets out armed with a good idea and an understanding of a likely failure but is willing to try.

The definition sure has its pokes but I honestly do not wish to achieve any ideals outside the functionality of this book as it suffices to guide *Our Entrepreneurship Mandate*.

Chances are that a good number of readers are aspiring or existing entrepreneurs while others are just on the fringes, deliberating if taking the plunge is a wise idea. I can tell you firsthand that entrepreneurship is a worthwhile endeavor; the joy of allowing your creative juice to flow unhindered and watching something you build from ground-up thrive, is a most rewarding pursuit.

Entrepreneurship is not without its demands, challenges, setbacks and enormous sacrifices, though rewarding in the long run as can be seen in the countless Success Stories even here in Africa, from the Cape to Cairo, there are more entrepreneurs smiling to the banks than ever in the history of the continent, and the space remains largely uncovered, yearning for more daring and discerning folks to take the plunge especially with impacts on a global scale.

WHO IS AN ENTREPRENEUR?

An entrepreneur as has been established initiates a new business, not necessarily a new idea or could be someone who collaborates on a new business idea with the attendant risk of failure; and is often the person saddled with pivotal roles and core operations or control of the company, especially at inception.

An up starter has no guarantee of success, no sure paycheck, no job security, or established system save his idea, passion and diligence.

Save for the entrepreneurial spirit that drives most entrepreneurs, it is otherwise often more convenient to get into an existing organization with established structures and operations, decent cash flow, and job security and possibly a jumbo paycheck and perks to go rather than try to set out without buffers or hope of success.

The road of an entrepreneur is uncertain and his map is unclear, many a times the zeal outweighs the realities, especially where there is limited start-up funds.

I dare say that it is not the paycheck that makes you an entrepreneur; it is the enterprise and your pursuit that sets you forth as an entrepreneur. I was listening to a radio program recently and a lady was sharing her experience as an entrepreneur, what caught my attention was when she said that for the first five years of her business she did not make Five Thousand Naira profit (at the current bank rate $25) and yet she kept at it. Her story has since changed but those harrowing 5 years today forms the fiber of her successful businesses.

You are not an entrepreneur only when you receive your first paycheck or cash, but right from the moment you set your heart, hands and your all to build a productive enterprise.

ARE ENTREPRENEURS MADE OR BORN?

Some folks are born entrepreneurs with a natural instinct for enterprise, while others are forged through life experiences: some folks from a young age have a natural inclination to trade, make stuffs, or just do something enterprising, while some have had to learn and become successes.

I strongly believe though that all humans are endowed with some measure of enterprising abilities which most times become dormant or stifled. Entrepreneurial Spirit can be stimulated and enhanced, as much as it can be suffocated in unfavorable circumstances. The unfavorable circumstances are not only adverse conditions, but we have come to see that wealth can suppress the desire to strive as with many folks from wealthy homes; as much as the hopelessness of poverty that besets creativity, the case I have observed in many African villages, little wonders that given the right environment, many Africans have gone on to excel in other more favorable climes.

Entrepreneurs are made and entrepreneurs are born. It is not coincidence that societies that favor entrepreneurs also happen to have high numbers of entrepreneurs, while societies with stifling policies also produce less entrepreneurs.

It is also interesting that the enterprising spirit has been known to flow uniquely in families, tribes and even communities. So, while entrepreneurial spirit can be innate, it can also be cultivated.

BRANDS OF ENTREPRENEURS

It takes a distinct set of persons to be entrepreneurs. Entrepreneurs may be diverse in their orientation and expression, but underlying attributes are same: they are folks that spot opportunity gaps and take the risk to commit self, time, energy and resources to make it an enterprise.

As you would have gleaned, there are entrepreneurs everywhere; all sectors boast of entrepreneurs, who make things happen, stimulate change and sometimes spearhead revolutions in the industry; Agropreneurs, Techpreneurs, Edupreneurs, Fashionpreneurs and as many "preneurs" as there are economic sub-divisions and industries.

However, my distinction is actually not focused across industry line, but motivation and the forms of activities and interests that births the entrepreneurs; regardless of what industry they belong. The distinction is about functionality; and analyzing the impulses that spur entrepreneurs. What inspires a person to start a new business in spite of the possibility of failure? I have come up with a list which I believe is not exhaustive, but it is very helpful and has more utilitarian benefits.

Sustenance entrepreneurs are a common sights in Africa where people participate in petty commerce with the aim of meeting their basic needs. The funds are so little that they mostly never go beyond one-man business for many years. It often entails trading in basic commodities; food stuffs and rendering essential services in the community. While this may seem meager, a lot of kids have been educated in sub-Saharan Africa from proceeds of sustenance enterprises. Kids are often co-opted to assist their parents in such enterprises. There is a lot that can be done to expand the capacities of these folks.

Community-based entrepreneurs are motivated by peculiarities in their community, which could be as a result of abundance of certain economic commodities or service that can be traded for income. Many dwellers of coastal areas have created activities from fishing, tourism, resort, and memorabilia around their community, while others with Shea, coconut, palm, Argan have developed highly flourishing community industries. Community entrepreneurship must be encouraged to control rural-urban migration, unemployment and provide easy access to economic activities in all local communities. At other times, entrepreneurs have taken advantage of deficit in their community to make money. It calls to mind the old tale of two folks who were sent by a shoe manufacturing company to assess a village they wished to explore for business. The first came back with a report that the folks don't wear shoes and there is no need going there; the other came back brimming with excitement about the enormous business opportunity that existed in a village where no one had shoes.

Perspectives may play a major role here. Imagine the gains that have been made by daring telecoms companies, who chose to invest in Nigeria at the turn of the new millennium. Bigger international players took the conventional knowledge of GDP, Per capita and other factors which were unfavorable, and ditched the idea of such investments, while the smaller companies that came to Nigeria focused on potentials and other unconventional considerations. The bigger boys made a huge mistake, realizing only too late once the "small boys" started posting international-attention grabbing returns in the telecoms sector. Community based entrepreneurs can achieve more with better understanding of opportunity.

Seasonal entrepreneurs create businesses to meet established periods of excessive demand, Xmas and other religious events, New Year, Nationally recognized days to cater for the surge generated on those days. Most seasonal entrepreneurs also have regular jobs or other income sources but cash in on the largesse of heavy-demand seasons. They also take advantage of periods of low demand to stockpile and hoard for later demand. I know several folks who keep poultry for the months preceding the Christmas only to make quick seasonal profit. Seasonal may be weekly, monthly, bi-monthly or any frequency that your endeavor requires and the turnover.

Passion (talent) entrepreneurs address folks who don't just have talents, but are able to harness their talents and often those of others into an income-generating enterprise; Musicians/Producer, Public Speaker/ Training others, Modeling/Agency, Dance/Group, Acting/Producing and Directing. You have often heard "turn your passion to profit". Your passion may be anything not limited to entertainment but you must be able to make it a profitable business. Examples are fashion designers, chefs etc. Turning a passion to business is as important as carrying out any other business. Your talents do not just turn into a business until you make an effective business model out of it. The better business details, the better the chances of good success; not all musicians who make money are entrepreneurs, and the distinction is clear from those who build ventures and structures around their talents.

Convenience entrepreneurs offer simplified alternatives to different life endeavors, by adding value to a process and charging for the value. Cooked & Packaged Foods, Pre-Cooked, Pre-processed, Various Brokers and agents in different industries, and all convenience that can bring the consumers' experience closer to the final state the client would desire. This would also include Shopping Agents and all activities buyers are willing to pay extra to get some ease or perceived advantage. Convenience Entrepreneurs have formed a symbiosis with large organizations to take care of non-core business operations. Convenience entrepreneurs make a living from offering simplified alternatives to different life endeavors.

Expertise entrepreneurs are very common, deploying their skill whether professional, artisanship or semi-skilled services. Emphasis that skill alone does not make an entrepreneur except the skill generates a new business, creates employment and wages for others over a period. Accountants and Finance experts, Lawyers, Medical Practitioners have been able to expand the frontiers of their profession by creating practices outside existing organizations that offer improved, varied, or other diversification in the industry. Fashion designers have created multi-million dollar businesses. African designers are doing pretty well, with many now showcasing on international runways. These skills are often acquired through trainings in formal, semi-formal institutions or through apprenticeships; barbers, hairdresser, and all professionals who have tangible application skills and venture into start-ups also fall into this category.

Industry Entrepreneurs are beginning to incite the coinage of "Intrapreneurship" with many folks tapping into gaps in their industry; some remain to service the identified market or subsequently break-away to establish new businesses. Intrapreneurs thrive in different sectors; Stylist have developed different hair products, Doctors have developed better tools for their practice, and Lawyers have devised means of Documenting Law Reports which have created a publishing business along their practice. Intrapreneurs are encouraged by discerning business owners to remain as collaborators rather than competitors because their aim is not to compete but to enhance a business process.

Social entrepreneurs Many of such entrepreneurs in the bid to solve society problems, environmental challenges, and correct defects in the educational sector, health sector or just about any field of concern have created solutions that people are willing to remunerate. A man in India invented low-budget, hygienic menstrual towels to help his wife and the women around him. The demand has spread to several communities who have similar concerns even outside India. Agriculture, maternal care, childcare, power generation and mass education have seen innovative concepts emerge. Social entrepreneurs do not start or base their dealings on profit making but it is a basic principle of entrepreneurship that people are always willing to pay for anything or service that solves a problem or adds perceived value.

Technology driven entrepreneurs are not necessarily technology-savvy or geeks. They might as well know next to nothing about the technology backbone of their business but they are able to develop businesses by deploying the existence of a technology. Without smart phones and all Computer-enabled devices, the social media and the global boom it is currently enjoying would be impossible or less successful. E- Commerce and blogs also ride on the internet technology, and it's been the same with previous technology evolutions where entrepreneurs have made a fortune. The businesses rest on being able to cash in on an existing technology.

Facebook founder adopted (and subsequently expanded on) the conventional paper yearbook and deployed it to the internet technology platforms making tremendous success of the idea. While this seems simple, one would wonder why no one else thought about it.

The first time I set eyes on digital camera I conceived a business idea. Photography was one of my pastimes and I just loved capturing many beautiful moments with my camera. I was in my 4th year studying Law when I approached a rich politician with a proposal to start a Digital Studio, I had never seen a digital studio or heard of any (we still went to the labs to develop our pictures and waited for days before we saw the photo, whether good or bad). "This is the future of photography" I told him as I gave him my quotation for the proposed new business which I did not have funds to realize. While I awaited his response, I started an apprenticeship with a Photo-journalist in my spare time, following him to events and gaining valuable experience in Photography. I never got my equipments, the loan or partnership as promised, rather the moneybag ran-off with the idea (Angel Investors is a concept that is still not formed in this clime and there is yet little value for intellectual property) It was really heartbreaking, but that's history.

Innovation remains the biggest raw material for entrepreneurs to tap into. All technologies known to man can be used to create a business opportunity.

Spontaneous entrepreneurs through their curious mind, tinkering with established systems, querying the order and reviewing the process eventually make a break.

Some of the biggest names are spontaneous entrepreneurs; Steve Jobs, the founder of Apple lead this pack in recent times. Now we have forgotten the days before introduction of apps, when we had to keep reloading the internet explorer to access emails and frequently used sites. A lot of inventions and innovations fall off these folks. I call them "The why not" entrepreneurs; there is always a progress that can be made on anything. Imagine the progress we have made from floppy disks, to CD Rom, USB and the sustained efforts in all fields of life courtesy of the numerous Bill Gates of this world who continue to reinvent technologies and tools, giving rise to new businesses. While they don't necessarily go out to do new businesses, their activities by itself are self-actualizing.

Serial entrepreneurs are never at a point of satiation. Sir Richard Branson may well be the father of serial entrepreneurs, with a passion for starting new businesses, charting new courses and just constantly on a next big project. serial entrepreneurs sometime have been known to sell off very successful business only to start-up another from the scratch. They are some of the most daring risk takers, who love the thrill of start-up challenges; many others have a plethora of businesses across different industry. Sir Branson of the Virgin Group coordinates 400 businesses across different sectors. He produces soft drinks, deals in books and music, owns a most successful airline among others. His latest project will take private individuals to space once it is completed. The premium juice of entrepreneurship runs through the veins of a serial entrepreneur: ideas are on daily basis.

THE MAKING OF AN ENTREPRENEUR

Being an entrepreneur has nothing to do with your personality but more with your inclinations and choices. It does not matter that you are an introvert or an extrovert. It is however certain that an entrepreneur cannot be a conformist; there must be a strong aversion to existing ideals, benchmarks and all "established" systems that smolder creativity, and innovation.

Societies that favor creativity, freedom and innovation often have more entrepreneurs than those that are averse to innovativeness consciously or otherwise. Little wonder much effort in recent times is going into ensuring ease of doing business in the bid to create an entrepreneur-friendly environment.

The verve in an entrepreneur does not fall in line, but often falls out of line because he is either seeing things differently, or ahead of others; he does not seat still in the boat and often might have to be thrown out or he just takes a dive.

The entrepreneur sees opportunities and does something about it. When Mark Zuckerberg 'got' the idea of Facebook he left school to pursue it understanding the importance of the opportunity and the timing in the new Social Media wave. I have heard folks ignorantly cite Bill Gates and others as examples of 'drop-outs' who eventually made it, and it's sad that many young folks with no concrete plans or idea formation have jettisoned their education hoping one day to find 'luck'. I can tell you for sure that entrepreneurship is not lottery; it is something far more than luck: these guys had all the pieces together.

They got something worth dying for and needed to concentrate on developing and making a success of the idea; they did not just take a blindfolded plunge off the cliff. Entrepreneurship is anything but brash and reckless. Most successful entrepreneurs are very calculated, deliberate and detailed.

STRATEGIC TRAITS OF AN ENTREPRENEUR:

Entrepreneurs have distinguishing traits that sets them apart. Many entrepreneurs share all or many of these compelling traits which are mostly forged through life lessons or learnt and practiced over time, a few folks are born with it though on the minority.

I often tell my staff that the essence of telling the stories I share is not to entertain, but to impart valuable lessons; if you don't differentiate between a story and a lesson, the value will be lost. A lot of folks have heard the same stories and have profited differently because of perception. There are attributes that are common to all entrepreneurs and these can be learnt. You cannot be an entrepreneur without effectively harnessing the traits.

 I have observed that most entrepreneurs have gotten more daring as they succeed. It tells me that, they did not start out with the whole success figured out; rather one success fuelled the appetite for more and another. It is also interesting that, the success of one person has served as a motivation for more people.

When you read a good success story, don't just leave it at a good story, take the lessons. The lessons will help you build your brain and brawn for better chances at success.

It becomes a strategic trait when there is a commitment to adopt and follow through to achieve the desired outcome.

It is a strategic trait for an entrepreneur to possess these traits:

STRATEGIC TRAIT 1

Be a visionary: A keen sense of imagination makes you to see things others do not see and it is the reason why sometimes it takes a while before your idea is accepted especially when it is a totally new idea or off the norm. You must see something that needs to be changed, improved, added, or modified within the existing order. Entrepreneurs don't just get over a challenge and be content; they go on to conceive solutions for others through it. Africa's richest Aliko Dangote did not just hear about the over 100 million units of Housing Deficit in Africa, he plunged into cement manufacturing and has conquered the Cement market in Nigeria, and West Africa and gone on to other parts of the continent to achieve similar feat.

STRATEGIC TRAIT 2

Be Proactive: An entrepreneur does not wait for things to happen, they make things happen. How many times have you complained about a problem in your community or about a need but you hoped someone did something about it. That is what entrepreneurs do; they "do something about it". Mosun Umoru is the new Queen of Nigeria's Agro-revolution; a university graduate taking to the fields to refine farming and food packaging and inspiring other young Africans to do same. Resourcefulness by far differentiates the lot who see the need from the few who eventually get to do something about the problem in good time.

STRATEGIC TRAIT 3

Be Passionate: You can never be a successful entrepreneur without passion. Passion is the fuel for your vision. Your zeal is so important that you cannot afford to run out on supplies. Passion in entrepreneurship is not the same as excitement as you may know it; a lot of times your excitement would wane especially when you encounter setbacks but it is your passion that keeps you going. That is why you must never run on another's passion; it won't sustain you for too long: imitation does not take anyone too far on the long haul of entrepreneurship.

A passionate entrepreneur is not propelled by his bank statement but his mind statement. Entrepreneurs may spend years from imagination to impact incurring losses, making blunders, running low and yet keep going because of the passion.

The story of Walt Disney is instructive in this; in spite of his interest in arts, he could not make it in prestigious art schools and only knew how to draw caricatures, with his fickle ability, he started drawing animations for a newspaper publisher who conned him because of his limited education. He created a rabbit character and unknown to him, he signed off the intellectual right to the character in his contract. He soon lost the rabbit character and his staff to the publisher. With no money to continue, he went in search of a job. He was so broke that he could not attend his job interview because his only shoe was held by the cobbler until he paid his debts. In the midst of this, he created the much celebrated Mickey Mouse character. Well over two decades after he set out to be an animator, he finally made his break. Today, several decades since the passing of Walt Disney, the Disney Entertainment Company still grosses over $40 billion annually.

STRATEGIC TRAIT 4

Be Focused: An entrepreneur is not the regular jolly good fellow. Building a business idea is hard work and mentally tasking. You must be focused to keep your eyes on the processes that will ensure the success of your business. You must remain focused in the face of criticism, cynicism, and praise. Focus would also require that you shut your eyes and ears from unprofitable distractions that would present themselves as alternatives to your vision, or modifications which may take you off the course of your vision. There is no harm in making a detour; but you must have a clear understanding of your decisions. It is very easy to get tempted to abdicate your own ship and join the merry band on another. That makes you a hustler not an entrepreneur.

Channels Television, Africa's most successful all news channel with operations in the UK, remains one of the continent's enviable enterprise with global appeal. The CEO shares in several interviews how he set out as a successful anchor from the government owned station to start his television station with little funds to pursue the big dream, Brick by brick and avoiding the distraction that came with an entertainment hungry viewership, the platform carved an enviable niche in Nigeria broadcasting and beyond.

Distraction no doubt remains one of the greatest setbacks of meaningful achievements for an entrepreneur. Many good ideas have been shipwrecked because of a loss of focus; The Titanic may be the best analogy here; without focus, the best ideas wither.

STRATEGIC TRAIT 5

Be Tenacious: As you execute your vision, take proactive steps, have your passion and focus intact, you must court tenacity: the ability to hold on; press on until you've achieved your goals. The time between your imagination and your impact may take days, weeks, months, and even years. The setbacks, the failures, the derision, the pressing needs in-between often demand a strong staying power to continue on the pursuit. The stick-to-it-ive-ness is a key ingredient lacking with many "failed entrepreneurs". The arm wrestle that entrepreneurs encounter against diverse challenges is the defining moment between those who finally succeed and those who crack up. Sometimes, to keep going, it may require that you took a paid employment as a stop gap or go through pupillage to crystallize the idea, but the ultimate vision must never diminish. Steve Jobs had to go that route, but kept his vision for Apple Inc.

STRATEGIC TRAIT 6

Be Purposeful: Entrepreneurs are people of purpose, not loafers. Entrepreneurship is not for folks who have nothing to do and decides to "just get into something"; that's a hustler. An entrepreneur sets out with a destination, a compass, and a map for his journey. While a hustler may join any train or ship, an entrepreneur cannot, because he is guided. In the same vein the hustler may well abandon route or pitch his tent anywhere that fits, an entrepreneur is made of deeper purpose and convictions.

Entrepreneurs are made of very thick ligaments which explain why most of the big names that have shaped history and those that are now shaping our world are entrepreneurs; it is not a play-safe zone.It is gritty, it is bumpy, it is simply gusty and only a keen sense of purpose can keep one going.

As you relish your Heinz ketchup, baked beans, mayonnaise and so many other Heinz delicacies, remember that it was almost buried by a bumper crop. There was actually a time when the name "Heinz" made grocers, farmers, and creditors livid because of H.J Heinz's huge bad-debt. Yet he remained convinced that as more women picked up formal jobs outside the homes and the economy continued to expand beyond the then peasant farming and industrialisation brought more urbanization, there would not be 6 hours to cook baked beans, pickles and other delicacies before every meal; with that purpose well established, he went on to rebuild his charred business. After years of slow and painful recovery, H.J Heinz came back stronger; bequeathing to the world numerous products and remains a billion dollar global enterprise till date.

SKILLS FOR SUCCESS

An entrepreneur must endeavor not to rely on just luck and chance; relevant and helpful skills must be acquired to ensure a successful enterprise.

Skills may be innate or acquired; although some skills can only be acquired. Baking, garment making, ICT and various kinds of vocation require that skills be acquired through varying period of learning,

Core Skill: If your business is tied to some specific skills and abilities, then you must endeavor to acquire the skill sets that will give you the best chance at sustainable success. It is very important as an entrepreneur to e the master of your game and continuously update your skills.

I caution very strongly against any attempt to build business where you have no competence for your core operations. If you must do any business; then you have to acquire the necessary skills.

Imagine a bakery owner who does not know how to bake. If you hire the best hand you can be sure that the business is over the day the expert leaves or gets a higher bid. Core skills are crucial to your long term success and other skills needful to complement your core business operations.

Other needful skills include the following and more:

Administrative skills: There is always some element of administration in all enterprise, no matter how little. It is needful to organize yourself, your staff and the business processes in order to maximize performance. This will require you to have a minimum understanding of cash flow, book-keeping, marketing, branding etc. You are starting from the scratch and may not be able to hire for the different needs, so you would need to equip yourself to be able to carry out several basic administrative functions at low budget. Administrative needs will continue to vary with the complexity of the business operation and there might be a need to hire, but hiring must be done to aid your operations, not to create a blind spot in your business.

Hard work is a skill as I have come to discover; the more dedication and efforts you are willing to put into your business the better the chances of success. Also, your staff (if you have any) would read your body language and unconsciously emulate you. As an entrepreneur, you cannot afford to be lazy; you will be required to do more than if you were in paid employment. If you cannot break your back to pursue your passion, no one else will.

One guy I admire so much is the CEO of Carlos Bakery in the United States, also host of the Cake Boss & Kitchen Boss TV Shows (I watch his show in Nigeria), I find it amazing that someone so accomplished still has his hands in the dough quite often. He is always in his chef's uniform and often times goes with the delivery truck in the back holding up the cake. It is never the way of Africans; we often find business proprietors here who get bigger than the business that brought them success in the first place, hence downslide in the quality of services and customer satisfaction. Always remember that your efforts will be amplified by your staff and so will your laziness.

Good Communication is important to your success, while you don't want to be held back by lack of good communication skills, you want to develop yourself on the go. When your business succeeds, you want to be able to tell your story.

ICT skill: It is also very important in this age. ICT is the language of modern communication and there is no excuse for anyone to do business in this age and time without deploying as much of the benefits ICT offers as can be utilized. There is so much to gain and there is so much to learn, but you can start from the basics and build up. Social Media has been deployed to build mega businesses. ICT is relevant for both internal and external operations. Even old businesses have been able to adapt their processes to the ICT platforms to maximize profit and save time. ICT cuts across all sectors of human endeavors, and is very useful at all levels of operations.

People management skills: This is very vital no business is an island: you will need to engage the services of staff as the business progresses and you will have to service people, one way or the other through your business; high-handedness and slackness with staff both have negative consequences and there is need to find a good middle point: no business exists without having to relate directly or indirectly with people. The new wave in customer relations now is not just that customer is King, but that your employees are now seen as the first customer of the business; a lot depends on them. They will project you, far more than you can control; so deal with them wisely. A lot of employees have been responsible for destroying painstakingly built businesses. The Entrepreneur is responsible for not just starting the business and employing staff, there must be a concerted effort to instill the right work ethics, values and ensure compliance by the staff; and of course the entrepreneur sets the example.

I have seen business owners bad-talk their clients with their staff without understanding that their little 'gist' does more damage to the business.

Reading and Continuous Learning must be a lifestyle especially in our ever changing world. Even the basest of man's need-food business has undergone severe changes in the way it is grown, processed, packaged and the understanding that consumers now have. You must watch and learn so that you can adjust faster to the times. Reading is the secret of the developed nations and world leaders; No wonder America has the highest number of bestselling authors in the world. A lot of entrepreneurs have been stalemated on one idea for two decades clinging on with little or no modifications or improvements, just the same things day in day out as long as there are buyers. It is a fatal place to stay for a business: death lurks around any business that has not changed, improved, diversified, or increased substantially over time.

STEPS TO ENTREPRENEURIAL SUCCESS

I have established that entrepreneurship is not a lazy, easy, quick chance endeavor, but a deliberate and dedicated effort at building an enterprise.

As with all buildings, there is no way out of ensuring that processes and procedures are followed from the get-go to eradicate and minimize failure. It is bad enough that the odds are already against a new start up until you scale the first five years, and the need to mitigate the risks of failure through well articulated steps. While the steps are not fool proof, planning in itself is an antidote to failure.

STEP 1

GENERATE BUSINESS IDEAS & ANALYZE YOUR IDEAS

Everything begins with your idea; whether new or modified, your idea is the soul of your business.

Ideas are the fulcrum of entrepreneurship development; without continuous ideas, entrepreneurship will cease. Generating ideas is not as simplistic as it may seem, neither is it a tough nut. But I realize that ideas do not come to those who don't seek ideas. Seeking ideas requires some concentration and interest. You have to engage your passive and active thought process until you get the light bulb moment, the illumination that will birth your business.

To guide you further in generating your Ideas:

i.   You must situate yourself in an interest or interests because there are ideas in every sector and you cannot possibly address all.

ii.   You must be a keen observer and look out for anomalies and gaps, needs, changes you can make, improvements and modifications in your sector.

iii. You must be an avid reader and pick as much information and interests as you can in your field. Your reading and research may take you outside your field of interest but must connect you to it.

iv.   You can generate loads of ideas and subject them to analysis. All successful folks have a brimming archive of failed ideas: before the CEO of Snapchat, Evan Spiegel got his break, there were other ideas he tried that never grew beyond the drawing board, while others made little impact.

v.   Not all ideas can be bankable, and not all the ideas you experiment will be a success, however to minimize the risk of failure, you must analyze your idea against important benchmarks by doing at least a SWOT analysis of the Strength, Weakness, Opportunities & Threats of the Idea. You can talk to a reliable enterprise consultant. Your SWOT must succinctly analyse the product or service against Need, Market analysis, Competition, Competence, Capital requirement, Profitability, and so on. You must read and research extensively to know policies and impending events that can affect your business.

vi.   Only when you have done a thorough job of getting a good idea, you move to Prepare for start-up. You don't expend money preparing until you are sure it is an idea worth pursuing.

I always advize people at this point of generating and analyzing to pick up some books; it is always helpful to oil your creative wheels by reading.

READING SUGGESTION

Think and Grow Rich - Napoleon Hill

How Successful People Think - John Maxwell

Several books out there and online resources that can boost your mind power for effective start-up.

STEP 2

PREPARE FOR START-UP

Your preparation starts with your paper and biro, or your electronic device as the case may be. You will need to dedicate creative moments charting a course for your business, which you will write out as you clarify the details and modify as the need arises.

 Taking this important step would move you closer to actualizing your idea and give you a sense of commitment. Anyone can dream up an idea, it is now time to design your dream as beautifully as you may. The future is said to belong to those who believe in the beauty of their dreams.

Success requires far more than a dream; the World's Chief Dreamer, Dr Martin Luther King Jr. Dreamt and acted for the emancipation of all races: so you must add action to your dreams.

I recall the experience of learning to drive and I know it is pretty similar with many folks; you just can't wait to get the steering wheel and zoom off, but you know that driving requires skill which will minimize mishaps. When you go through the driving school, you prepare for the big moment when you actually have your license and hit the road. From desire to reality, there is a necessary preparation, and all the preparation only pays off when you actually hit the road.

 Preparation is important for your start-up and the better prepared you are, the better your chances at success. Imagine all the efforts that big companies put into making a new product from inception to the consumer?

Many entrepreneurs fail to make this all important preparation because they do not differentiate between hustling, pastime and entrepreneurship.

Entrepreneurship is not just about a good idea worth trying, because in the event that it "fails" do you stop being an entrepreneur? An entrepreneur is not made by one attempt but mostly by perseverance and several attempts.

Entrepreneur don't just do it to invest their money into something, there is a higher compelling interest than investment and returns; the zeal to build. It is ok to be an investor, but investing alone does not make you an entrepreneur, if you are not the forerunner or strong hands (risk-taker) behind the business, then you are not an entrepreneur. This factor also differentiates from managers employed in many businesses; a manager can resign, or get fired but an entrepreneur is the soul of the business.

Entrepreneurs do not 'do it to keep busy' as we have seen the rich folks who set up businesses for their wives and kids without a care for returns or results as is mostly the case in this clime.

Entrepreneurs don't ride on with just doing what they enjoy doing for only as long as they enjoy it, because many of the challenges ahead will be anything but fun, yet the passion keeps them going.

It is a tough job to build and sustain a viable business.

Entrepreneurs don't just do it to make a living, but to fulfill a burning passion; even though the option to take the faster route of paid employment exists.

The process of being an entrepreneur is the beginning of many tough and uncertain days; entrepreneurship does not guarantee free time and less work; reverse is the case because you will need to work at least twice as hard for your own course and put in more time, though flexible; you will make more sacrifices which will take time to materialize.

Having set that forth, and you have psyched yourself up for the business, you must do the groundwork even if it is your 10th venture with 9 successful ones behind you. Mark off the following as mandatory to your preparation:

1. **Regulatory compliance**: You might need to register your business and fulfil all regulatory requirements incidental to the business. You will require a solicitor for this and other statutory experts. Be mindful that some specialized industry requirements and safety considerations may affect your own industry; Financial Institutions, Education, Health, Food & Beverages, and Professional Services have stringent requirements.

2. **Intellectual Rights** safeguards might be needful, also with the assistance of your consultant or solicitor to protect your concept from infringement.

3. **Make a business Plan;** If you get a professional to put one together for you, make sure you have very strong inputs because you are the one to implement it. Your plan must reflect your interest and the core of your idea (your unique selling proposition) as would be workable for you. More will be discussed on business planning in later details.

4. **Create a business model** that will work for your idea which will be reflected in your product/services, mode of operation, packaging or the area where you highlight your unique business advantage. Your model must place emphasis on your uniqueness to adequately distinguish you in the market

5. **Gather your resources**; acquire space if needed, equipment, team, funds and all details.

STEP 3

BUSINESS PLANNING

I take for granted that entrepreneurs at this level have an idea of what a business plan is; that document that is the blueprint of your business? Having dispensed that, the question about the importance of business plan writing subsists. Many folks have asked if there is need for a business plan, some even give examples of businesses that do not have a plan and in spite are successful.

For whatever it is worth, a lot of businesses have run successfully without a business plan; however, research continues to lean in favor of writing one; reflecting that Businesses with business plans have better chances at succeeding than those without. It makes business sense to give your business the best possible chance for success and do all to clarify all ambiguities as you set out.

The Advantage of having a business plan includes;

- Helps to harness and articulate your thoughts
- Subjects your idea to thorough and further scrutiny
- Throws up areas you might have omitted in your analysis and avails you the option to review your ideas before further execution
- Holds you accountable to your ideas

- The plan gives potential investors an opportunity to analyze the details of your idea coherently, which might not be possible otherwise.

There is no hard and fast rule to your business plan writing and a lot of guidance is on the web now. You don't need to lift ideas verbatim, because you might not be able to defend or execute it if you don't have your brain input in the whole process.

When I was an Awardee in a Competition at the Nation's Capital several years back in a Business Plan Competition, I realized that the more I progressed in the different phases of the Competition, the better I could visualize and execute on the concept, by the time the finals came, I had so much understanding of the business than I could have imagined possible at inception. Business Plan is to an entrepreneur, what a building plan is to a builder, it might take some efforts to create, but once done, the work becomes easier.

When you create your Business Plan, ensure the plan includes the following:

- An executive Summary, which gives a quick overview of your idea, and can be extracted for your elevator pitch, and other quick presentations.
- Your Management Framework and operation structure
- Your Product or Service analysis

- Market Analysis, to consider potential customers, and competition
- Your Sales Strategy
- Your Financial Analysis, particularly your cash flow.

Endeavor to have originality and clarity of thought in writing your business plan; it is for you first before the investors and other stakeholders.

READING SUGGESTION

How to Prepare a Business Plan- Edward Blackwell

STEP 4

OPERATING STRUCTURE

You must create an operating structure for your business and inculcate same into your business plan, no matter how simple, which should be reinvented as the business grows.

Home-based business is a structure, and entails creating a workspace, work time and clear distinction from personal life. A lot of folks have created successful businesses from home and the challenge arises only when you cannot clearly separate your business equipments, time, supplies, resources, and staff from your home use. It makes tracking cash flow and workflow difficult.

Your operating structure will be determined by the nature of business, clientele/niche, market forces, available resources and time. You may chose to adopt:

Office/Outlet operations

Multi-level Marketing model

E-commerce Platforms

Drop-off sales

Open Van

Referral based etc

You may choose to adopt more than one, but all are not appropriate in all circumstances. So also in structuring the production method whether it is to be outsourced or in-house; staffing may be part-time or full; wages or commission as suitable.

Detail is one thing that too many people do not wish to be bothered about, especially in our fast age; you cannot go wrong on details as long as you don't become so soaked in the details to the detriment of your business operations. Too much detail, like too much of anything may be detrimental to your business; there is need to strike a good balance between too much and too little details, to avoid undue loss of time.

Once you have the operating structure figured out, it is good to commence operations immediately.

STEP 4

TEAM BUILDING

You may be able to start business on your own, but you will need to expand as the business grows.

your team is as important as you, especially those who play key roles in your operations. Businesses have been ruined by the team, while some have been able to carry on effectively even at the demise of the pioneer.

The team include: the pioneer, the staff, the board (who are sometimes only advisory due to their wealth of experience) and may include other key collaborating organizations.

As succinctly as I can put it, make sure you build a disciplined and happy team; Let them understand and share your passion and you must continually keep them on course. Your team is made up of humans who have feeling and interests just like you. You must ensure that your team share a sense of belonging in your vision and feel your genuine concern for their interests and welfare. Oprah Winfrey has taught the world a thing or two about team building, based on basic principles of the golden rule: do unto others as you would want done to you (*tibi vis fieri, alteri ne feceris*). Your team must be empowered to carry your vision effectively in and out of your presence.

STEP 5

MARKETING YOUR BUSINESS

At the point of marketing your Business you must have put all your ideas in place and you are now at the view of the public, you will need to present your business attractively; in a compelling and persuasive way.

Never forget that you are the first marketer of your business and the first customer too. You might need to bring on a good dose of innovativeness; this is where your doggedness would be most tested.

I read sometimes back that the first attempt at making the now billion-Naira industry for sachet water in Lagos was a failure, majorly due to over 100% mark up on the local water people were used to buying before the "pure water" was introduced. The manufacturer had to go to Ibadan at the University where people bought in on the "new idea from Lagos" because they saw Lagos as the national pace setter. The fact that it came from Lagos got folks from other states in Nigeria who are obsessed with all things Lagos to buy them; like the global crave for All Things American. The sachet water business has since gone on to penetrate Nigeria and beyond with thousands of proprietors cashing in on it now.

Marketing is the life of your business, and that is where all your ideas and resilience gets tested. You must be optimistic and yet reserve a little thought of a possible unfavorable outcome.

Do not define the success of your idea by only a single marketing approach or market segment, time, location, or presentation; try across diverse options and give time and take surveys and feedbacks serious but not personal, so that you can gain valuable insights for improvements where needful.

The market is a loud and tough place. You will be confronted with various challenges but you must endeavor to rise above them. When you eventually gain a good spot in the market you must strive to maintain it through continuous quality business practices.

STEP 6

GROWING & SUSTAINING GROWTH

When your business starts to grow, you must do all to sustain the growth. All the good practices you started with are always best maintained.

Avoid getting carried away with the success to a point that you are unaware of impending problems. Maintain healthy relationship with your staff and never hands-off the core of your operations. All the details should be at your fingertips, remain relevant and current, and watch out for competition and anything that may halt your cruise. Don't be content to be a one product success, because any unavoidable change will mean you are out of business; add value, add innovativeness and never settle.

STEP 7

CHALLENGES AND MITIGATION

Challenges are the hallmark of an entrepreneur; when loss, failure, setback, breakdown, weariness, mounts, the true entrepreneur gets going.

Entrepreneurs are like the mythical bird in the Greek mythology- the phoenix that burns completely to ashes and soon rises again from its ruins. It seems like a pretty good story, but I have encountered that personally countless times and I am still at it. Living in a society that places little premium on intellectual efforts is particularly disheartening.

Nigeria and most African countries rank very poor in "ease of doing business"; It is by far easier to draw a paycheck and save yourself the headache of trying, but something deep inside has kept me going all these years. In fact the disappointments outweigh the successes, yet I keep pressing.

Folks come to my office and on the face of it term it as success, nice neighborhood, a decent facility and all the things that seem plush, but to me are far from my idea of success. I have had several ideas stolen by money bags who in other climes would be "angel investors". I have been exploited by highly connected folks to develop very successful ideas which I never got a slice of the bounty. Some ideas have died for lack of funds to pursue but I have never reclined my convictions that entrepreneurship pays ultimately.

It would have been good if I listed possible challenges, but it is a waste of time: challenges will differ in context, in severity, in climes and all possible variations. What is similar to all is that with determination and a die-hard mentality you can succeed as many folks have and still do everywhere in the world.

The best way to handle whatever challenges is to analyze the problem, and use the lessons as a launch pad for better performance; regrets or surrender has never been a solution.

Like Thomas Edison, appreciating that there are ways which won't work; does not mean there is no way at all. Never let any challenges snuff out the flickers of your passion rather you get it burning brightly with the gush of your resolve; oxygen can put out or ignite a fire, know how to use failure and setbacks to ignite your flames.

It is good to understand that the entire process is a learning curve. There is no Business School that will adequately prepare you for all the challenges, in business you will build your muscle on the field and learn faster by practice. That is why developed worlds place premium on experience not paper qualifications.

Challenges are the gym of entrepreneurs; only the best come out fit and stronger.

PART II

THE 10 DYNAMICS FOR ENTREPRENEURSHIP DEVELOPMENT

The 10 Dynamics for Entrepreneurship Development are based on insights gained over the years; practicing, supporting, training, researching and maintaining keen interest in entrepreneurship.

If entrepreneurship has been identified as the new economic order for economic growth by all leading economies, then we must do more to develop practical framework to maximize the benefits.

It is only by entrepreneurship that regular fresh graduates, college drop-outs and folks who are not heirs to any fortune can within half a decade feature on the Forbes Billionaire list.

Left to the giant corporations, a lot of big economies would be in roil and turmoil, since the turn of the millennium, but for millions of new start ups mopping up the labor market and ensuring the creation of new wealth.

Holistic development, adaptable across different economies, societies and of contemporary application is what the 10 Dynamics postulate.

As we encourage the populace old and young, male and female, citizens and foreign to embrace entrepreneurship and focus less on white-collar jobs, there must be comprehensive, concerted and continuous efforts as identified in the 10 Dynamics.

In my observations, the absence of qualitative merchantable skills or know-how and basic business education have left many entrepreneurs overwhelmed and frustrated. In other cases, enthusiastic entrepreneurs have been inundated by financial challenges, government policies, seclusion, lack of support mechanism and many subtle but equally important factors that have sapped the passion of many.

The 10 dynamics is helpful not by the vast volume of information, but in being able to condense major touch points for entrepreneurs, governments and stakeholders in Africa and beyond. Entrepreneurship development must be tackled as a multi-headed issue and approached from different sides to create entrepreneurially vibrant societies.

A look at the cycle below shows the 10 focal areas that the government must pay keen attention; the 10 dynamics are interdependent approaches to bolster long term entrepreneurship development. They must be concerted and well articulated to achieve marked results in entrepreneurship development.

THE AFRICA ENTREPRENEURSHIP AGENDA

The Africa Entrepreneurship Agenda outlines propositions needful for the development of Africa, through a collaborative and integrated entrepreneurship development framework.

Africa beckons like a country lass; plain, unattractive and devoid of sophistication but inherent is the raw and feisty beauty that lies in her,, awaiting to be tapped, harnessed, and revealed by only the discerning..

 Africa today holds many distressing records of underdevelopment, but we have come to appreciate from recent success stories around the globe that development can be replicated effectively. Development is a Science.

I have come to realize that there is no magic in development; Singapore, China, The UAE, South Africa and many of the newly developed economies in Asia are proof to what determination, good governance, collective and concerted efforts can achieve.

The Africa Entrepreneurship Agenda proposes a plethora of methods necessary to achieving accelerated entrepreneurship development in Africa.. It is my true belief that where economic activities increase;, poverty and all its kindred can be effectively decimated.

In Morocco the fortunes of many local women turned around after years of local consumption and use of Argan (an oleaginous plant native to Morocco, Africa) in impoverished huts was replaced with the prosperity that the new global demand for the oils and sundry affords. In many areas, and regions of Africa,, economic activities have catapulted ailing economies while jumpstarting some others from the very scratch: When Dangote cements (now with over $20 Billion market capitalization) acquired the Obajana Cement Complex, in the remote village in Kogi State,, Nigeria there was very fickle presence of economic activities in the area. Now things have changed pretty much with the thousands of heavy duty trucks hauling cements across the country from Obajana., earning a spot in the Forbes Top 5 listed companies in West Africa.

The Stories of potentials and outstanding success remains true for many who have ventured to unravel the hidden treasures in Africa,. Africa is a green field for entrepreneurs, and investors, tasking but very rewarding.

The Agenda is to stimulate sustainable development in Africa through grassroots economic activities. The local communities, the municipals, small cluster groups, cooperatives and sole proprietors forming the bedrock of entrepreneurship drive for Africa through deliberate engagements.

DOING BUSINESS IN AFRICA

To do or not to do business in Africa; remains a critical consideration particularly for foreign Investors, and daring young entrepreneurs who crisscross the globe daily in search of new opportunities. Africa to most of these folks is just the perceptions drawn from media reports, which have not particularly served Africa well.

Africa is home to over 30% of mineral resources and raw materials in the world, with a strong presence of numerous Fortune 500 companies.

23 of the Forbes Global Billionaires in 2016 are Africans, living and doing business in Africa.

Yes, Africa has been setback owing majorly to bad leadership, there is yet a lot of opportunities for Entrepreneurs in all sectors. Africa is still largely an export and resources driven economy, importing most finished products. Discerning entrepreneurs can begin to tap into Africa's growing economies to provide goods and services that would otherwise be imported.

Nigeria features prominent in the global consumption of champagne and other luxury goods, with over 170 million people, International Entrepreneurs should focus on the perks and benefits of a new opportunity in Africa through: manufacturing, Services, ICT, Technology, Agriculture,

Retailing, Entertainment and Recreation, Real Estates, and numerous areas.

Administrative, Policy and other anti-investor challenges are receiving effective attention now , while many Investors have gone on to conquer the terrain adapting local sense.

There is no better time than now, as more African countries are more focused on their development and the need to diversify from export-driven economies.

THE 10 DYNAMICS FOR ENTREPRENEURSHIP DEVELOPMENT

People-centered policies and action plans; of the people, by the people, for the people is the core of the 10 Dynamics for Entrepreneurship Development.

1. ENTREPRENEURSHIP CENTERS

Without Entrepreneurship Centers, there would be ineffective development of entrepreneurship in Africa. These centers may range from basic Entrepreneurship Centers that function in the communities to advanced and research- enabled centers in tertiary institutions.

Entrepreneurship Centers vested with the responsibility of coordinating entrepreneurship activities are very crucial to the development of entrepreneurs, especially in Africa where formal education is still very low, with a high percentage of the population between 16-65 years uneducated.

The Entrepreneurship Centers must set out with clear understanding that both highly educated and otherwise can access entrepreneurship development., especially at the community level.

The Centers that currently exist are a far cry from the demands of the digital age. It is no longer just enough to set up a building with furniture and a few equipments, but attention must be given to the details of quality and sufficient equipments which would be constantly upgraded and replaced for maximum efficiency.

Entrepreneurship Centers should be created as close to the communities in proximity, and operations. The well-trained staff and well equipped centers must be engaged with a view to effectively propagate, administer and manage entrepreneurship development in the communities with very specific and empirical mandates backed by effective monitoring.

Nigeria with an estimated 170-180 million people and a landmass slightly below 1 million km sq, administered through a centralized Federal Government, 36 Federating States, and 774 Local Government Areas is the most populous nation in Africa and the 7th across the globe. It requires that there must be at least 1 Entrepreneurship Center in each municipality: 774 well-funded, well-staffed and trained, and well equipped, Entrepreneurship Centers for the drive to be successful and impactful. These numbers can be increased where distances between some of these municipalities exceed 3 hours travel time and with consideration to population density.

States should set up coordinating structures and the Federal Government have specialized agencies with focus on policy, research and development at the national level.

This model can be adapted to suit different countries and localities.

Many of the Entrepreneurship Centers in the Continent have continued to record very negligible impact in Entrepreneurship Development, while the Privates have done significantly better.

The failings (failings in terms of impact) of many of the existing entrepreneurship institutions in this part of the world rest on the following factors:

1. Entrepreneurship cannot be spearheaded by non-entrepreneurs: Career civil servants who draw paychecks and have never undertaken any enterprise cannot have appreciable understanding of entrepreneurship. Many Entrepreneurship Centers in Nigeria are staffed by career civil servants, whose best understanding of entrepreneurship is what has been studied or acquired through courses.

   Studying business and doing business are certainly poles apart; few of the rich folks here in Africa and the world have MBAs, and very few MBA holders own any of the biggest businesses in the world. Entrepreneurship is not what can be read without hands-on exposure.

   The situation becomes more pathetic and impossible where public servants (operating in a bureaucracy) are vested with the all important duty of developing entrepreneurs.

   Public employees can never develop entrepreneurs; they are poles apart in orientation, inclination, disposition, motivation and convictions.

2. Entrepreneurship has not been accorded the needed priority attention: Not due to the fault of the handlers, whose limitations were earlier set-out, the policy makers must deliberately going forward accord due and uttermost importance to sustainable entrepreneurship development. Good funding must be earmarked to stimulate the process. The

attention of the governments of most African countries is still very weak in that direction, even in the face of recent global surge. There is nowhere in the world where the governments are committed to youth empowerment, poverty eradication, fighting unemployment and bridging gender gap is entrepreneurship not given a prime place in policy directions: Africa cannot afford to do otherwise.

3. Conventional Bureaucracy is antithetical to entrepreneurial spirit: The Entrepreneurship Centers should be established with grants, and run on the same lane as non-profit organizations. They must be able to generate income, work independently, deploying the fundamentals of entrepreneurship that they teach. My early formal training in Entrepreneurship was at an agency of government whose staff drew paychecks at the end of the month from government coffers, smiled into seminars and workshops with well-structured PowerPoint presentations. I remember saying to one of the facilitators years down the line that I will never be taught entrepreneurship by bureaucrats again: they have never known to painstakingly toil and anxiously wait for no definite time before the yields come. An entrepreneur, sharing on a radio interview said she ran her business for 5 years before the first pay check arrived; you can hear that in a School: there is always the unwritten code.

I guess that throws light on why many bureaucrats who ventured into business after retirement get severely burnt?

4. Emphasis on only vocational training, without basic business management training:

After observing the high turnover of trainees at most of the "Youth Empowerment Centers" and the feeble attendant results, I realized that there was an important gap in their training which left many of the trainees clueless as to how to turn their skills to businesses. I drew up a Module that addressed the basics of Business Plan Writing, Book Keeping, Marketing & Sales Small Business, Business differentiation techniques, Financing for Small Business, Challenges & Mitigation and other Business Management skills, to be delivered at no fee with a registration of N200 ($1) (*learning from experience never to give any training free because it is never good for the recipients' psyche, even $0.1 is more effective than nothing. Entrepreneurs must learn to place value on their development). I approached a Local Government with the proposal to offer the 1 week long module to their Vocational Center, which had over 200 students going through different skill acquisition programs; I was rescheduled a few times for appointments that never held for one reason or the other until my altruism waned.

My concern as I have observed time and again was just that vocational skill alone was not enough and does not translate to making an entrepreneur.

That being said, a good entrepreneurship center must be set up with a mandate to ensure maximum achievement of entrepreneurship development opportunities.

A good Entrepreneurship Center should in addition to qualified and effective personnel have:

- A modern seminar room which can also double as a common room at rest times
- Well-equipped Vocational Rooms, partitioned for specialized vocations(baking, garment making, ICT etc)
- A Starters Hub that will serve as an incubator for greenhorns to be able to start their businesses in a controlled environment with minimum cost
- ICT Center & Library
- Administrative office and Support facilities

The Entrepreneurship Center will run trainings for both management and Vocational training using in-house experts and external resources at controlled cost.

The Center must be able to carry out basic Research and Development activities with a view to expand operations and maintain relevance.

The Center shall serve as a training and administrative front for research and development efforts aimed at entrepreneurship and economic development.

The Center should have a functional entrepreneurship hub that will create effective focal units along industry lines to promote incubation process for budding ideas, support start-ups and guide sustainability. Continuous education through seminars and workshops for established entrepreneurs will also be a regular part of the Centers' activities

Each Center must be positioned and equipped to be able to adopt the general template to develop its own unique potentials with recourse to its peculiarity; urban-rural consideration, infrastructure, culture & heritage, available resources both tangible and intangible.

This list is not exhaustive, but I believe the direction is clear.

Stimulating economic activities should be the main drive of the Centers; imagine the embarrassment of a well-endowed country like Nigeria, obtusely stringed to only oil and gas as the stay of the economy, in spite of very rich deposits of Minerals and Agricultural potentials.

The population strength of Nigeria can be charged for fantastic economic advantage if well harnessed and developed for productivity as China has proved to the world.

Same applies to our water bodies, waterways, extensive arable lands for both food and cash crop in a country that spend billions of Dollars annually importing staple foods. Tourism and hospitality can be another major economic driver as Kenya, Dubai and other climes have proved. Our abundant vegetation, forest resources and raw materials which are still substantially dormant, can decongest the urban Centers bloated with unproductive workforce.

The Entrepreneurship Centers must be so vibrant as to be able to identify, stimulate and develop new frontiers for business opportunities.

2. ENTREPRENEURSHIP EDUCATION: VOCATIONAL & MANAGEMENT TRAINING

Entrepreneurship is now a discipline and must be treated as such at every level of learning.

Many Universities in advanced countries now have up to Postgraduate Degrees in Entrepreneurship. While we cannot expect everyone to attain to that level, the minimum education an entrepreneur must possess in this time is a good vocational training or skill enhancement training and mandatory basic management training. This is particularly helpful where we have a high population that are not lettered but who can still be developed for productive enterprises.

For societies in Africa that are still on the verge of sustenance entrepreneurship, life-changing practical skills should be the focus, which the recipients are expected to build upon for economic advantage.

Vocational trainings are borderless, cutting across people of different educational background and socio-ethnic leanings.

While impacting vocational skills, care must be taken to appreciate that the essence of the vocational skill is not to stifle creativity, and must encourage expansion of knowledge and diversification like every form of education.

Immediate efforts can be explored in the following areas, with the all important agriculture sector taking the lead, modules should be developed that will incorporate a rich practical experience with minimum theory inputs to make hands-on application the focus:

- Agri & Agro-allied

- Manufacturing & Cottage Industries (Household chemicals & personal care)
- Artistry & Crafts (Beads, Hat, Bags etc)
- Body Care & Enhancement
- Events Management
- Foods: Baking & Confectionery
- Foods: Catering & Culinary Skills
- Foods: Processing & Packaging
- Furnishing & Interior & Exterior Decoration
- ICT- (Web Design, Repairs, etc)
- Photography & Video Techniques
- Publishing and Book Industry
- Service Industry
- Shoe & Leather Works
- Tailoring & Fabric Works (Adire etc)
- Life application Services
- Talents to Profit Group
- Cluster group Businesses and lots

Vocational skills must be thorough and give regards to safety and public regulations, presented with ethics and understanding of environmental and public interest.

Management skills on the other hand confer on entrepreneurs intangible resources, which are mandatory for managing a profitable business especially in the 21st century. Several vocational skills have not translated to good business ventures due to lack of management skills, there is therefore no doubt that all successful entrepreneurs require soft skills in their business endeavors which would invariably translates to business success.

The Basic management courses include:

- Introduction to Business & Entrepreneurship Sensitization

- Elementary Bookkeeping & Business Finance

- Legal & Regulatory Issues

- Personal Development & Business Ethics

- Success Tips – Marketing, Packaging and Presentation, Customer Relations, Competition & Survival and more

It is also an inexhaustible list and really, management training is a lifelong pursuit as your business grows so also the need to make changes that will influence how you do your business. There will also be specialized trainings for specific industry, new tools and facilities and such adjustments as may follow occasional feedbacks, research and survey.

START-UP AID & SUSTAINABILITY SUPPORT

In addition to the trainings, the entrepreneur would require support and buffers.

Even in the minutest form, support can bolster the confidence of the entrepreneur as we have observed over time that several brilliant ideas never see the light, for fear to venture. Atychiphobia (or playfully I call"Start-upophobia") has kept many entrepreneurs from venturing, and no word is true for an entrepreneur than "Nothing Ventured; nothing gained". Venturing is easier said than achieved especially seeing that life is littered with intentions that were never actualized.

In addition to receiving encouraging cheers from the sidelines, the Entrepreneur will do well with practical and effective supports that would take him closer to his goals.

While this does not guarantee success, it sure gives a better chance at success, as have been observed with Cooperative based businesses.

There is no support too much to give a start-up, be it financial, technical, informational and research, professional or otherwise. It can be deduced from the OECD records that Entrepreneur-friendly countries have recorded more successful startups than others, and it is no surprises that US, UK, France, and Canada are on the top 10. Countries like South

Korea have introduced interest rates below 2% to encourage access to finance for starters.

Cooperative Groups have been discovered to be a very viable business model in rural Africa, hence more businesses are being encouraged to form Associations around Products, Services, Localities and access bulk funds and low interest grants. These Local Associations help to monitor members' progress and provide a platform for accountability, review, discipline, and cross- fertilization of ideas.

Taiwan has developed policies that supports and actively finances manufacturing, while some other countries offer tax exemptions, grants, rebates, actual government- guarantee, mentorship and amended policies to encourage start-ups. Our Francophone neighbors, Togo and Benin have done some things differently thus making the ranks of most improved countries for doing business globally; they have focused on easing regulatory issues for Starting a business, securing certain permits and cross-border businesses.

Government and Policy makers must pay close attention to policies that drive or stifle entrepreneurship development, and be careful with wholesale importation of Regional and International Treaties and Conventions inimical to indigenous success, especially Economic Partnership Agreements that are inimical to the growth of Indigenous

African Businesses. Regulatory bodies should be positioned to guide and safeguard businesses and not be a stumbling block in the way of starters.

The Corporate Affairs Commission (CAC), (the body vested with business registration in Nigeria) have turned back lots of names at Incorporation for no justifiable reason forgetting that in these times, new businesses are as good as their identity, same with the cost, time and bottlenecks involved the CAC processes which are often very crippling.

Big corporation should in no way be allowed to trample on the up starters; it must be a collaboration that gives the big corporation no advantage to place barriers to entry or survival of startups.

Research institutes, data banks & the educational sectors must continue to generate new vistas for possible endeavor. In the absence of which there will be too much duplicity of the little available know-how. When the market for cottage production of household chemicals opened about 10 years ago in Nigeria, it was a viable means of income for many households and a good number of them went on to gain statewide and regional spread. In recent times however , the proliferation has led to a decline in the value and viability of the industry.

Suffice to say that new ways must continually be developed, new ideas through our academic and research institutions to sustain start-ups. These institutions also help to test and validate new ideas against available data, statistics, production, safety, proprietary interests, competition and other viability tests. This gap is a major disadvantage to start up where data and information are absent, obsolete or grossly inadequate in most of Africa.

Development agencies are as much involved in start-up supports. The efforts of The World Bank Group, UNDP, USAid, DFid and numerous iNGOs remain commendable against the background of poor infrastructure, high illiteracy, language barrier, volatility, and ominous challenges. A lot more can be achieved once well-meaning locales are trained and frequently re-trained with the continued support of the Development partners and stakeholders.

Much has been said about the Entrepreneurship Centers and it is easy to see the pivotal role they can and should play in supporting startups for sustainable growth. Above all, an entrepreneur must make good use of all support because he alone holds the key to unlock his potentials: a ton of support cannot amount to much with a disoriented and unwilling individual.

Sustainability Support

Starting a business can be gratifying; there is however a need to sustain the business and ensure that it grows to maturity. The gloomy statistics that only 30% of businesses are still a going concern at the 5th year can be mitigated using a combination of bespoke solutions to sustain the enterprise; continuous education, financial support with expansion funds, mitigation of exigencies among others.

Sustainability is as important to the entrepreneur as it is to the society: it is the business of all concerned that except for grounds of mismanagement and unethical practice, we all must ensure that as many businesses stay afloat, grow and continue to expand. It might seem meager, but a sole proprietor with only 5 staff who also have dependents; pay bills, educate and cater for their kids and family may have more burden added to the community if the means of livelihood is lost.

Particular attention here goes to a lot of employees who through sharp practices have sucked businesses of well-meaning entrepreneurs aground.

It is a very common occurrence for employees to devise means of side-cutting their employers in the bid to make some quick bucks, or gain unethical advantages. The temporary benefit has never been worth the pain of watching businesses go down, leaving several people stranded and dreams dead.

The sad reality in Nigeria and several African countries that there are no third generation businesses and very few 2nd generation businesses; most businesses die with the initiator and many manage to survive briefly, before folding up.

Economies like UK and even the United States have sustained their lead in the Global Economy by the many Businesses that have been passed down through several generations and have spread to other countries of the world, beyond the pioneer's imagination. Sustainability must be at the heart of the drive for entrepreneurship development if meaningful impact would be made. Finances as it affects sustainability would be addressed in details under that rubric.

COMMUNITY OUTREACH ADVOCACY AND PROGRAMS

As a law undergraduate I came across entrepreneurship as a discipline through a dear mentor who invited me for a seminar and without doubt it has been a lifetime impact.

Yes, I loved to trade, and tinker with petty enterprises around me for as long as I could remember. As a child I made neighbors pay a token to pick fruits from the numerous trees that dotted our compound and at some point I had peppered meat and toasted bread out with our security guard (called aboki) as I went off to school in 9th grade, I returned from school every day to pick the little proceeds from my small enterprise. All the while, I never knew there was anything called entrepreneurship. As a law student, a short distance adjacent the University, I had reached a little arrangement with the owners of a bookstore to pick books at an agreed discount, and with a little markup on their recommended retail Price I sold to my colleagues in the classroom. Valentine season was another cash cow for me with the added services of making deliveries across hostels. Those and several ideas I explored before I ever heard the word "entrepreneur" and so it was an aha! moment when I attended that seminar that validated my proclivity to commerce.

Community outreaches are very effective in Africa where the Village Square culture is still very active. Several government initiatives in different sectors have garnered grassroots approval using the Community outreach method.

Workshops, seminars, conferences, and other programs aimed at entrepreneurship development must continue to be propagated even more than ever. Entrepreneurship programs have helped a lot of people secure good livelihoods and fulfill passions that would otherwise remain dormant.

Until recently, Start-up was a taboo for graduates in Nigeria; it was the norm that once you are a graduate, you go on to secure a job in the public sector, big organizations or somewhere in the organized private sector. Only when you have tried all that, and failed at it, stayed back home for upwards of 2 years can you consider or voice the idea to your parents about setting out alone; it was not honorable and no one wanted it; entrepreneurship was a no-no; it was considered for no-goods. This perception has since changed as the awareness is spreading and more success stories are recounted.

Many folks now resign voluntarily from big organizations to start-up, and professionals have crossed careers and fields to pursue their passion for fashion, baking, teaching, manufacturing, micro-journalism, with men and women interchanging gender-dominated fields.

It is awesome seeing new industry created by the effort of a trailblazer; less than a decade, professional makeup was unknown in this clime, but today it is a core of all events, with some organizations engaging in-house makeup professionals, while several make-up professional have set up independently, raking in good businesses from weddings, parties, shows, model works, the movie industry and individuals. Much of the credits for this go to Tara Durotoye, a pioneer of Professional Makeup Industry in Nigeria, who has since established numerous training centers and created her makeup line alongside her advocacy and mentorship efforts.

The makeup market in Nigeria alone directly engages over a quarter of a million, both male and female as more programs, seminars, workshop, are organized.

The same can be achieved in other markets and industries. Community outreaches must continue to form part of the mass impact activities.

5. EFFECTIVE COLLABORATIONS: MENTORING & COUNSELING, PEER REVIEW & NETWORKING

Collaboration is now more important in business than competition, especially for SMEs. Working with others at different and diverse levels of operations is key to developing a strong entrepreneurial culture. The era of "eat alone, die alone" is no more the way to go: entrepreneurship does not need to be a lonely walk in the dreadful wilderness.

While it is important to collaborate and encourage collaborations, the emphasis rests on the effectiveness of the process to ensure that the business gets the benefits: collaborations with experts for mentoring and counseling, with peers for reviews and appraisals and networking to expand contacts and business opportunities.

Business clinics among other benefits provide a platform for check up, diagnosis and necessary prescriptions to help entrepreneurs maintain a healthy business, while counseling inures from mentorship.

The value of mentorship has not been properly explored, and it is imperative to revive the pupillage culture in Africa, which enables transfer of life-skills from mentor to protégé in an informal and yet effective way. Protégés are advised to take advantage of the wealth of experience of their mentors rather than seek monetary benefits.

I understand that all business pioneers are entrepreneurs, but there are lines of distinction often forged along lines of commonality in business and levels of operation. The Peer Review forums will provide a platform for players within similar industry, equal or contiguous levels of operations to deliberate on issues of common business interest, with a view of enhancing profitability, and effective business practices.

6. CONDUCIVE FINANCIAL FRAMEWORK

Finance is yet the bane of most entrepreneurs' aspirations. I wept at a training I was facilitating in Kaduna State some years back when a woman of about 50 years old, wizened more from poverty than her years told me that she had attended a training to make local bath soaps and wash soaps but could not get capital to start the business. The capital was a mere N20, 000 ($100) which she was unable to raise since most of the folks in her community were equally poor or poorer.

In most of the challenges I have seen, finance ranks overwhelmingly the most, and it also happens to be one of the easiest to tackle directly. I also know of a certain woman who required the same amount to start a Crayfish trade where she got about a 100% turnover every 3 days. Once her business started, she was able to send her kids to school and give decent meals.

Imagine how many folks in Nigeria and rural Africa can benefit from $100-$200 unconditional cash transfers? Other methods that do not require direct cash are the Leasing Option, stock-inputs etc.

Financial Institutions in Africa must be remodeled to serve the very grassroots. Financing of SMEs is so critical that special and concerted attention should be paid to Micro Finance Institutions. Most Microfinance Banks in Nigeria are still operating on double digit interests making it very difficult for SMEs, as well as tough conditions to accessing funds with minimum impediments. There have been suggestions that the Land Use

Policy be reviewed to enhance the fiscal values of the lands as security for loans.

Loans in most cases have become burdens more than offer help to the entrepreneurs, due to high interests, insufficient moratorium period to enable proper consolidation of the business. Financial illiteracy also affects much of the populace in Africa, both the educated and the unschooled; most defaults are due to financial illiteracy than to recklessness.

Angel Investors are a very rare sight in Africa as most entrepreneurs have fallen prey to shark investors, who prey on start-ups. I have been a victim and many other entrepreneurs have been mauled.

There is no meaningful development that can happen without a conducive and favorable financial framework.

7. INTERVENTION & STIMULUS PROJECTS

In order to stimulate entrepreneurial activities in many communities in Africa, there will be need to undertake different intervention projects with focus on special interest groups such as women, youths, communities, special skilled people, cluster groups and post-rehab persons using a bespoke approach.

I read extensively about the Argan Production Projects in rural Morocco, which are Community enterprises developed around the locally available Argan tree, its oils and fruits. The Argan was discovered to have much cosmetic properties and pharmaceutical uses and had the peculiarity of being able to thrive only in that locality and nowhere else in the world. Several industries with the help of the government and other bodies have since sprung up at different level from cultivation to processing. Stimulus Projects are not limited to just agriculture, to locality or interests. People have been taught skills; groups have been transformed into a cluster through Special Intervention Schemes. Kwali village in Abuja remains a significant pottery town due to the activities of Mrs Ladi Kwali, a foremost Potter and with the timely intervention of efforts to spread the interests to the locales.

GOVERNANCE & POLICY

The last few years have seen tangible changes in many countries in the bid to create entrepreneurially-conducive societies. As mentioned, the gap between entrepreneurially vibrant economies and others will widen if there is no deliberate policy thrust.

America was quick to see and respond to the new wave of people-driven economy, and the result is evident today. The compass of active and fundamental research carried out before the turn of the millennium pointed to the ensuing end of the industrial revolution (industry-driven economy), where the economy was then shaped and steered by giant corporations and the public corporations.

As technology increased, and international outsourcing was embraced, the manpower requirements also reduced which required downsizing for operational efficiency, with the decrease continued till date aided by the new dimensions in ICT. America was able to navigate this slippery curve by encouraging and empowering start-ups, and I bet it is the best discovery America has made since Coca Cola. While Big Corporations retrenched in thousands, startups employed in millions, contributing significantly to the overall economy of the US.

It is therefore in the best interest of all governments to continue to develop entrepreneurs to meet the immediate challenge of unemployment and curb redundancy in the productive populace. While that remains the big picture, governments must also zoom in to several underpinnings of entrepreneurially enabled societies; with Facebook launched, and tremendously successful, it was not long before Twitter, Whatsapp, Instagram, Snapchat and a torrent of very successful social media platforms also made their worth.

The Silicon Valley in California boosts of the most new wealth created in the US in recent years, where very young Technopreneurs rake in Billions of Dollars from across the globe. In similar strides, China, India, Europe and others are effectively steering a people-driven economic order with highly commendable outcomes across sectors.

That being said, there is no doubt that any government that is committed to fighting poverty, unemployment, hunger, disease, illiteracy in the 21st century must make entrepreneurship a top priority. Entrepreneurs must be encouraged in all sectors to drive the grassroots economy; several employing one or more persons and helping to reduce the weight of unemployment which itself is a major policy concern.

While entrepreneurship is a people-driven economy; the paradox requires effective policies, government interventions and enabling environment, better infrastructure and power supply among others that rests on the government will and commitment especially in Africa.

The government must understand its important roles in achieving an entrepreneurship-friendly society and be deliberate in a committed and painstaking effort to encourage and develop entrepreneurs.

WHAT EVERY RESPONSIVE GOVERNMENT IN AFRICA MUST DO

- Re-order its priorities to align with the current global realities.
- Make firm and very effective policies, commit resources for entrepreneurship development
- Develop a sustainable vision for orientation and reorientation of the people to inculcate entrepreneurial values.
- Create enabling environments and incentives for Entrepreneurs
- Inculcate entrepreneurship in curriculums at all levels of education. I only got to hear about entrepreneurship as an undergraduate and a lot more only recently with the increased awareness.
- Youth Corp Services (1 year service mandatory in Nigeria for Graduates) and all such schemes in other parts of the Continent must be reinvented and directed to Entrepreneurship, Agriculture and Teaching opportunities
- Specialized schools should be created for entrepreneurship
- Use and encourage strong media participation in entrepreneurship development efforts.
- Tackle entrepreneurship as a broad-based issue, deploying the 10 Dynamics highlighted in this book and as many more.
- Seek international collaborations with folks who have successfully created working models

- Selfish and greedy ambitions must be sacrificed for the common good, to foster qualitative, competitive and conducive growth in the sector.

It is important to spearhead and support policies geared at promoting the growth of Entrepreneurship and condemn anti-entrepreneurship policies that directly or indirectly hamper the development of Entrepreneurship.

The policies of the government can no longer relegate entrepreneurship issues. The policies must be proactive, robust and deliberate to address all the issues that affects and concern entrepreneurship development at all levels.

CONVENTIONAL MEDIA & ICT TOOLS

Entrepreneurship must be accorded policy priority on the mass media. There must be an active, deliberate and conscientious effort to disseminate entrepreneurship with the same or higher commitment the Entertainment and Soft sell stories are done.

The power of Radio, other conventional media, social media and all veritable ICT tools must be widely explored to enhance the goals and objectives of entrepreneurship development.

Having featured frequently on radio programs and the recently on TV, I have no doubt that the radio remains a most veritable tool for community engagement in this part of the world.

More of the rural populations still depend largely on their radio to connect with the world. In the hustle and bustle of Lagos, where much of the populace spend upwards of 5 hours in traffic daily, the radio from 5am-10pm is at its busiest.

Social media has come to stay, with more young people getting on the different platforms. Millions of youths can be captured through effective messages and information on these platforms. Blogs should be encouraged to include entrepreneurship contents in their publications.

RESEARCH AND DEVELOPMENT

R & D remains the invisible hand behind much of the developments in the rest of the world. Entrepreneurs all over the world are not often the ones who carry out researches; they just spot an opportunity in a science research or any other sector and synthesize it to a business.

Research and Development must be broad and diverse to address different sectors of the economy. R & D is the love child of academics in different fields of endeavor. In the Food Supply chain for example, there are researches that starts from the seed, through the cultivation and harvesting, to storage, processing, till it ends on the consumer's' table. Imagine all the fallout of enterprises in that sector alone produces, per variant of uses and opportunities discovered and the excesses they now have to export?

Translate that reality to ICT, Finance, Real Estates, Medicine, Retailing, Mining, the other Services Sector, and you have a robust, broad-based economy with different levels and inclinations of entrepreneurs driving the entire process.

Research and Development duties of Institutions have been neglected leading to dearth of local information. R & D is a continuous effort which must be continued to help maintain societal development across sectors.

A PROTOTYPE STANDARD ENTREPRENEURSHIP CENTER

Part II talks extensively about the Entrepreneurship Center, Structure, Management, responsibilities and operations.

This Prototype is a Model Center that gives estimation for a standard Entrepreneurship Center, with a take-off grant of $200,000, fully realizable within 5 years of operations, and at least 2000 successful entrepreneurs in the period.

Agege Area of Lagos State, Nigeria would be our benchmark:

1) The building: Spacious and preferably not shared.

   i Seminar Rooms (At least 2-3) 50-100 user capacity, collapsible, soundproof walls.

   ii. Vocational Rooms (for practical & equipments) 20-50 users

   iii. Resource Center (ICT and Library) 30-50 user

   iv. Lounge/Cafeteria

   v. Recreation Area

   vi. Starters Hub (20 meet & Greet Booths)

2) Equipments
   i.   Fully Installed & Integrated Desktops for offices, Resource Center (15 units)

ii. Laptops

iii. Projectors & other computer components

iv. TV & Sundry

v. Furnishing & partitioning

vi. Practical & Vocational equipments & Tools

vii.　Other equipments

3) Vehicles

i Bus

ii Truck

4) Others

i. Staff remuneration for first 6 months

ii.　Curriculum & Modules Development

iii.　Take off costs

iv.　Miscellaneous

Income generation opportunities for the entrepreneurship center includes:

i.　Students enrolment

ii.　Consultancy services

iii.　Periodicals & Publications

iv.　Facility rentals

v.　Workshops, Exhibitions, & Seminars

vi.　Merchandising

vii. Starter-Hubs (Meet & Greet Booths)

viii. Resource Center , Lounge and Cafeteria income

ix. others

CODA

Entrepreneurship is

The dream of all;

The dare of some;

The reward of few

~ 'Ola- Grace

POSTSCRIPT

THE NOUVEAU PRENEUR AGE

Months after my manuscript was in, the idea of the *Nouveau Preneur* clicked. It seemed a petty idea at first, but soon expounded in my mind as a concept worth of note and of course sharing.

The *Nouveau Preneur* epitomizes the new wave of entrepreneurs that are springing up from every corners of the globe, Africa inclusive: the *Nouveau Preneur* may not necessarily be doing something new, but is certainly doing something in a new way.

The *Nouveau Preneur* understands the secret of the times and taps into the opportunities for gains. ICT has revolutionized the way we live, work and play, and there is no way of stopping it.

ICT has brought us into a digital age, where devices and platforms are now the closest ways to get to people. Most people now spend all their waking hours in the company of devices, even more than they are with other folks. The *Nouveau Preneur* is Uber, Air BnB, Indiegogo, Instagram, Alibaba.com, M-Pesa of Kenya, MWeb of South Africa, Budget of Nigeria, Jumia and Konga Online Stores, the Bloggers and too numerous to mention Startups recently tapping into the infinitude of the Internet and Global Connectivity.

The Industries and interests no doubt differ, but the ICT backbone that defines the success of these ideas often creates a contemporary flare, with very far reaching opportunities.

When E-BAY, Amazon and some of the earlier e-commerce sites started out, it seemed like a good idea, with most businesses conceding the ICT platforms as another Marketing option. That puny assumption has changed now as the realization sets that, the Internet is not just a good option, but is the new age. The Blogs have also come and all the Social network sites have continued to expand and modify the prospects within the new realities of ICT opportunities.

ICT is no more an option, it is a whole new vista, it has brought life experiences closer to humans, and it will be very difficult or impossible to imagine that humans would go back to the days when you could not do much at fingertips.

The *Nouveau Preneurs* understand that life experiences are now at the fingertips; just a click or touch away, and anything further does not suit the Nouveau Preneur Age.

The *Nouveau Preneur* is the person who can bring life experiences closer, easier, faster, preferably within already existing digital experience. I am not talking about the Hi-Tech, Digital-savvy giants; my focus is on folks who use little ICT inputs, components and basic devices to create a whole new business and living experience.

In the last few years there is almost nothing that has not been conceived as an app, and the numbers are growing each day, offering a plethora of fantastic services through the Phones and Tabs.

While on the face of it, all may sound exciting, I wish to drop a note of warning to the entrepreneurs, especially aspiring entrepreneurs who may often not understand that with start-ups and indeed all businesses, there is always a carrot and stick: It is never a winner take all situation. It is hard work that takes time and all the issues discussed in the Preceding Chapters. The *Nouveau Preneur* is not perched on the Islands in the Bahamas, or enjoying the Suntan in Dubai for most of the year, scrolling phones and sipping a Tropical mix, while the cash flows in; in fact the easy life enjoyed by service users is much more than that at the backend of the service providers. It requires a lot of unending strategic thinking, planning and jiggling to become and remain in demand, it is as any other business that can be birthed and nurtured, that can grow and that can die with poor management et al.

On a global scale, the *Nouveau Preneurs* are the highest employers of labor in recent time and offer yet the greatest dynamics to our living experience in recent times. It is the *Nouveau Preneur* Age; From Games to Real estates, to medicare, Professional Services, Education and all, the opportunities of this age beckon, waiting to embrace all-comers.

Africa has a pocket of indigenous success stories; yet, there remain enormous frontiers to grab global spots. Africa needs to invest more in educating the youths for this Digital Age. ICT has become an exportable skill; and it is currently one of the critical skills that give Asia a competitive advantage in the Global Labor Market, where Africa on the other hand falls short considerably.

ICT skills are more than browsing, owing laptops and tabs. The Digital Age just like the schooling system has levels and parameters, which most Africans have been known to operate far beneath the baseline, in spite of several years of exposure to computers (it is safe to conclude that most African have minimum appreciation of the dynamics of the Digital age beyond the basics, which would continue to be a big disadvantage if nothing holistic is done).

The Digital Age is in top gear, Entrepreneurs in Africa and elsewhere must re-strategize, re-equip and re-formulate for international relevance. Without a clear understanding of the Digital Age and its vast offerings, there can be no *Nouveau Preneurs* to drive 21st century entrepreneurship in Africa at full verve.

www.ingramcontent.com/pod-product-compliance
Lightning Source LLC
Chambersburg PA
CBHW022020170526
45157CB00003B/1298